Decodable
Takehome
Books

Level 1
Core Books 1–59

A Division of The **McGraw·Hill** *Companies*

Columbus, Ohio

www.sra4kids.com

SRA/McGraw-Hill

A Division of The **McGraw·Hill** *Companies*

2005 Imprint

Send all inquiries to:
SRA/McGraw-Hill
8787 Orion Place
Columbus, OH 43240-4027

ISBN 0-07-572305-0
        12 13 14 15 16 17 18 19 QPD 06 05 04

Table of Contents

Level I Core Books

About the Decodable Takehome Books

The *SRA Open Court Reading Decodable Books* allow your students to apply their knowledge of phonic elements to read simple, engaging texts. Each story supports instruction in a new phonic element and incorporates elements and words that have been learned earlier.

The students can fold and staple the pages of each *Decodable Takehome Book* to make books of their own to keep and read. We suggest that you keep extra sets of the stories in your classroom for the children to reread.

How to make a Decodable Takehome Book

1. Tear out the pages you need.

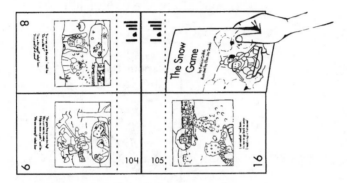

2. For 16-page stories, place pages 8 and 9, 6 and 11, 4 and 13, and 2 and 15 faceup.

or

2. For 8-page stories, place pages 4 and 5, and pages 2 and 7 faceup.

For 16-page book

3. Place the pages on top of each other in this order: pages 8 and 9, pages 6 and 11, pages 4 and 13, and pages 2 and 15.

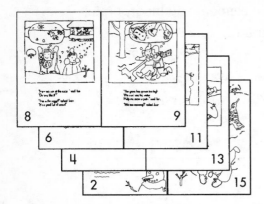

4. Fold along the center line.

5. Check to make sure the pages are in order.

6. Staple the pages along the fold.

For 8-page book

3. Place pages 4 and 5 on top of pages 2 and 7.

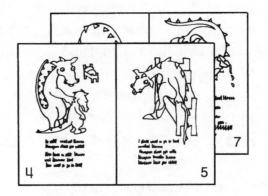

4. Fold along the center line.

5. Check to make sure the pages are in order.

6. Staple the pages along the fold.

Just to let you know...

A message from _____

Help your child discover the joy of independent reading with *SRA Open Court Reading*. From time to time your child will bring home his or her very own *Decodable Takehome Books* to share with you. With your help, these stories can give your child important reading practice and a joyful shared reading experience.

You may want to set aside a few minutes every evening to read these stories together. Here are some suggestions you may find helpful:

- Do not expect your child to read each story perfectly, but concentrate on sharing the book together.
- Participate by doing some of the reading.
- Talk about the stories as you read, give lots of encouragement, and watch as your child becomes more fluent throughout the year!

Learning to read takes lots of practice. Sharing these stories is one way that your child can gain that valuable practice. Encourage your child to keep the *Decodable Takehome Books* in a special place. This collection will make a library of books that your child can read and reread. Take the time to listen to your child read from his or her library. Just a few moments of shared reading each day can give your child the confidence needed to excel in reading.

Children who read every day come to think of reading as a pleasant, natural part of life. One way to inspire your child to read is to show that reading is an important part of your life by letting him or her see you reading books, magazines, newspapers, or any other materials. Another good way to show that you value reading is to share a *Decodable Takehome Book* with your child each day.

Successful reading experiences allow children to be proud of their new-found reading ability. Support your child with interest and enthusiasm about reading. You won't regret it!

SRA Open Court Reading

A Table

by Amy Goldman Koss

illustrated by Susanne DeMarco

Core Book 1

SRA

A Division of *The McGraw-Hill Companies*

Columbus, Ohio

9

8

2

A !

dog

7

A  is on the  .

ball   table

A is on the .

mug   suitcase

4

A

newspaper

is on the

ball

.

5

A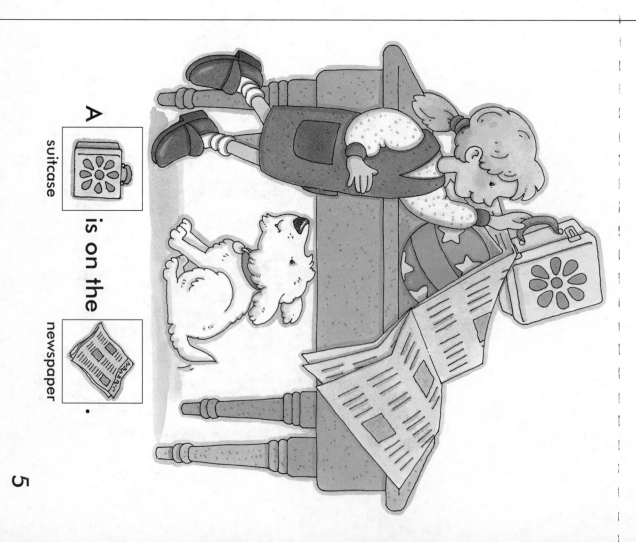

suitcase

is on the

newspaper

.

OPEN COURT READING

The Egg

by Amy Goldman Koss
illustrated by Olivia Cole

Core Book 2

SRA

A Division of The McGraw-Hill Companies

Columbus, Ohio

In the 🥚 WAS a  .

egg   bird

www.sra4kids.com

SRA/McGraw-Hill

A Division of The McGraw-Hill Companies

Copyright © 2002 by SRA/McGraw-Hill.

All rights reserved. Except as permitted under the United States Copyright Act, no part of this publication may be reproduced or distributed in any form or by any means, or stored in a database or retrieval system, without prior written permission from the publisher.

Printed in the United States of America.

Send all inquiries to:
SRA/McGraw-Hill
8787 Orion Place
Columbus, OH 43240-4027

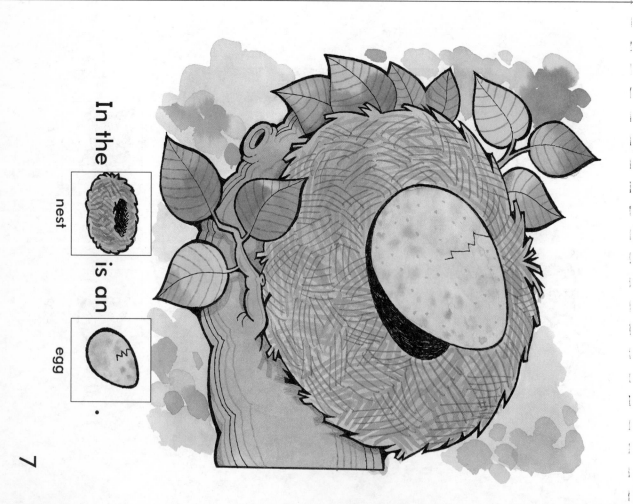

In the nest is an egg .

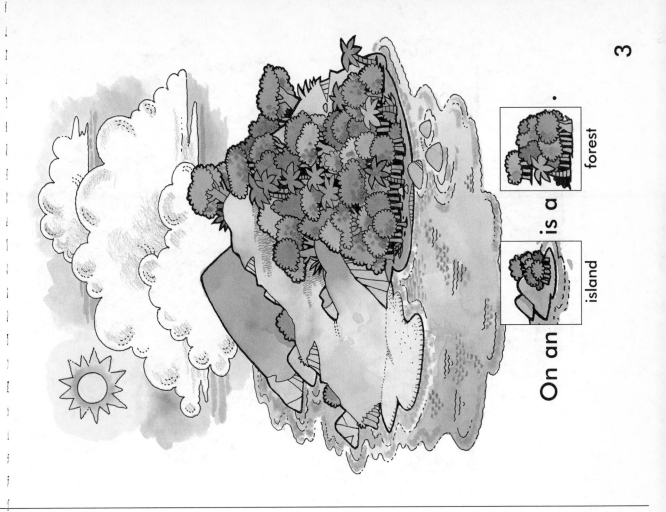

On an ⬚ is a ⬚ .

island   forest

3

On the ⬚ is a ⬚ .

branch   nest

6

4

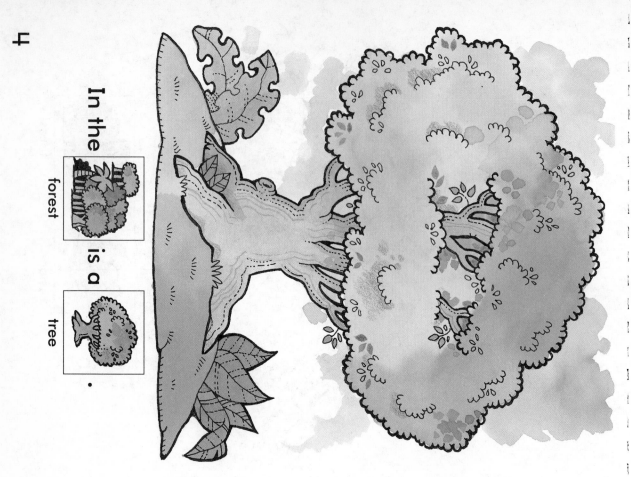

In the is a .

forest   tree

On the  is a  .

tree   branch

5

The Baby

by Amy Goldman Koss
illustrated by Sylvie Wickstrom

Core Book 3

A Division of The McGraw-Hill Companies

Columbus, Ohio

17

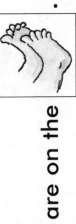

The ☐ are on the ☐ .

socks   feet

16

www.sra4kids.com

SRA/McGraw-Hill

A Division of The McGraw-Hill Companies

Copyright © 2002 by SRA/McGraw-Hill.

All rights reserved. Except as permitted under the United States Copyright Act, no part of this publication may be reproduced or distributed in any form or by any means, or stored in a database or retrieval system, without prior written permission from the publisher.

Printed in the United States of America.

Send all inquiries to:
SRA/McGraw-Hill
8787 Orion Place
Columbus, OH 43240-4027

The 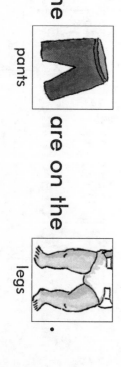 are on the  .

pants   legs

The Cake

The  baby is in the 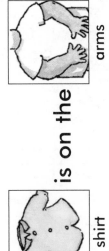 chair .

The 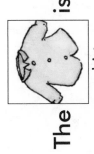 shirt is on the arms .

19

3

14

The

cake

is on the

ear

.

4

The

socks

are on the

hands

.

13

The | is on the | .

cake | nose

The | are on the | .

pants | arms

6

The

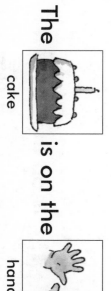

cake

is on the

hands

.

The Shirt

22

The

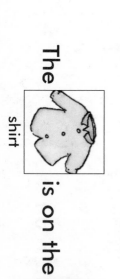

shirt

is on the

head

.

11

The  cake is on the girl .

The girl is in the tub .

The baby is in the tub .

Mom and I

by Tim Paulson
illustrated by Olivia Cole

Core Book 4

A Division of The McGraw-Hill Companies

Columbus, Ohio

www.sra4kids.com

SRA/McGraw-Hill

A Division of The McGraw-Hill Companies

Copyright © 2002 by SRA/McGraw-Hill.

All rights reserved. Except as permitted under the United States Copyright Act, no part of this publication may be reproduced or distributed in any form or by any means, or stored in a database or retrieval system, without prior written permission from the publisher.

Printed in the United States of America.

Send all inquiries to:
SRA/McGraw-Hill
8787 Orion Place
Columbus, OH 43240-4027

2

I make a

card

.

27

 makes

 toast

and

 jam

.

3

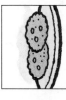

Mmm

 cookies

!

6

4

Mom

makes

cereal

and

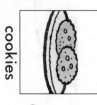

juice

.

Mom

makes

cookies

and

milk

.

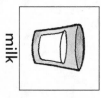

5

Sam, Sam, Sam

by Linda Cave
illustrated by Meryl Henderson

Core Book 5

SRA

A Division of The McGraw-Hill Companies

Columbus, Ohio

I am Sam.

8

www.sra4kids.com

SRA/McGraw-Hill

A Division of The McGraw-Hill Companies

Copyright © 2002 by SRA/McGraw-Hill.

Printed in the United States of America.

Send all inquiries to:
SRA/McGraw-Hill
8787 Orion Place
Columbus, OH 43240-4027

Sam, Sam, Sam.

I am Sam.

3

Sam?

6

I am Sam.

I am Sam.

Open Court Reading

Matt and Sam

by Martha Wood

illustrated by Olivia Cole

Core Book 6

SRA

A Division of The McGraw-Hill Companies

Columbus, Ohio

33

Sam sat on a mat.

8

www.sra4kids.com

SRA/McGraw-Hill

A Division of The McGraw-Hill Companies

Copyright © 2002 by SRA/McGraw-Hill.

Printed in the United States of America.

Send all inquiries to:
SRA/McGraw-Hill
8787 Orion Place
Columbus, OH 43240-4027

2

Sam sat.

7

Matt

3

Sam

6

4

Matt sat.

Matt sat on Sam.

5

37

A Hat

by Amy Goldman Koss
illustrated by Susanne DeMarco

Core Book 7

A Division of The McGraw-Hill Companies

Columbus, Ohio

A ham!

8

www.sra4kids.com

SRA/McGraw-Hill

A Division of The McGraw-Hill Companies

Copyright © 2002 by SRA/McGraw-Hill.

Printed in the United States of America.

Send all inquiries to:
SRA/McGraw-Hill
8787 Orion Place
Columbus, OH 43240-4027

2

A ham in a hat?

7

In a hat is a .

ham

6

Matt has a .

hat

3

In a hat is a  rabbit .

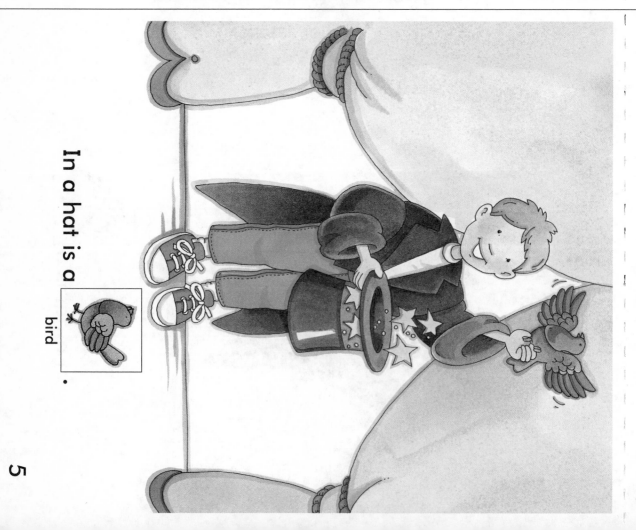

In a hat is a bird .

The Map

by Lucy Shepard
illustrated by Olivia Cole

Core Book 8

SRA

A Division of The McGraw-Hill Companies

Columbus, Ohio

41

Pam's map!

8

www.sra4kids.com

SRA/McGraw-Hill

A Division of The McGraw-Hill Companies

Copyright © 2002 by SRA/McGraw-Hill.

Printed in the United States of America.

Send all inquiries to:
SRA/McGraw-Hill
8787 Orion Place
Columbus, OH 43240-4027

2

Sam pats Pam's map.

7

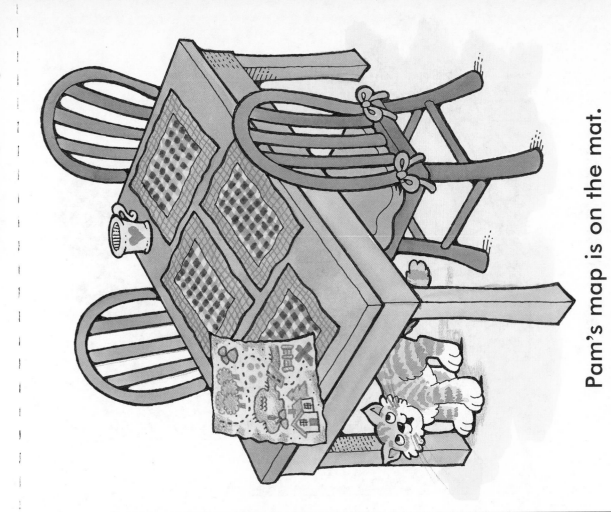

Pam's map is on the mat.

3

Sam taps Pam's map.

6

43

4

Pam taps the map.

Sam stamps on Pam's map.

5

45

Hip

by Nancy Thomas
illustrated by Len Epstein

Core Book 9

A Division of The McGraw-Hill Companies
Columbus, Ohio

Hip sits.

2

Hip hits his hat.

7

Hip has a hat.

3

Hip stamps.

6

Hip tips his hat.

4

Hip taps.

5

49

Open Court Reading

Snap the Ant

by Nicole Michael
illustrated by Len Epstein

Core Book 10

SRA

A Division of The McGraw-Hill Companies

Columbus, Ohio

Snap naps.

2

Snap is by the pants.

7

Snap is an ant.

3

Snap sips.

6

Snap is on Pam's pan.

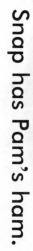

Snap has Pam's ham.

SRA OPEN COURT READING

Lil's Hat

by Linda Cave
illustrated by Deborah Colvin Borgo

Core Book 11

A Division of The McGraw-Hill Companies

Columbus, Ohio

53

Lil's hat is on Hal.
Hal's hat is on Lil.

8

Slam! Lil hits Hal.

Hal has a slim hat.

3

Hal sits and makes a list.

6

4

Lil is Hal's pal.
Lil's hat tilts.
It slips.

Lil slips down, down, down!

5

SRA Open Court Reading

A Mill on a Hill

by Jen Richards
illustrated by Jan Pyk

Core Book 12

SRA

A Division of The McGraw-Hill Companies

Columbus, Ohio

A tall mill is still.

www.sra4kids.com

SRA/McGraw-Hill

A Division of The McGraw-Hill Companies

Copyright © 2002 by SRA/McGraw-Hill.

All rights reserved. Except as permitted under the United States Copyright Act, no part of this publication may be reproduced or distributed in any form or by any means, or stored in a database or retrieval system, without prior written permission from the publisher.

Printed in the United States of America.

Send all inquiries to:
SRA/McGraw-Hill
8787 Orion Place
Columbus, OH 43240-4027

2

A tall man tilts.
A tall man tips.
A small plant on a sill tilts and tips, too.

7

A tall mill sits on a hill.

A small man taps a tall man
who sits in a mill.

A tall man sits in a hall in a tall mill.

4

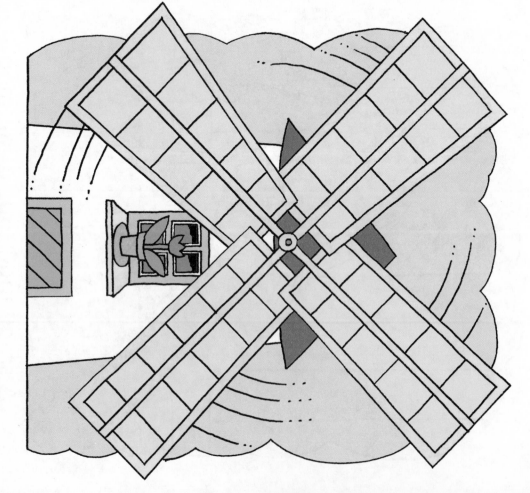

A small plant sits on a sill.

5

SRA Open Court Reading

Nan's Family

by Anne and Robert O'Brien
illustrated by Linda Kelen

Core Book 13

A Division of *The McGraw-Hill Companies*

Columbus, Ohio

I can!

Nan spins a tin pan!

16

61

www.sra4kids.com

SRA/McGraw-Hill

A Division of The McGraw-Hill Companies

Copyright © 2002 by SRA/McGraw-Hill.

All rights reserved. Except as permitted under the United States Copyright Act, no part of this publication may be reproduced or distributed in any form or by any means, or stored in a database or retrieval system, without prior written permission from the publisher.

Printed in the United States of America.

Send all inquiries to:
SRA/McGraw-Hill
8787 Orion Place
Columbus, OH 43240-4027

Can Nan spin a tin pan?

On the Mat

Sam sits on his mat.

Nan hits and tips the tin pan.

14

4

Pat sits on Sam.

Tim spins his tin pan.

13

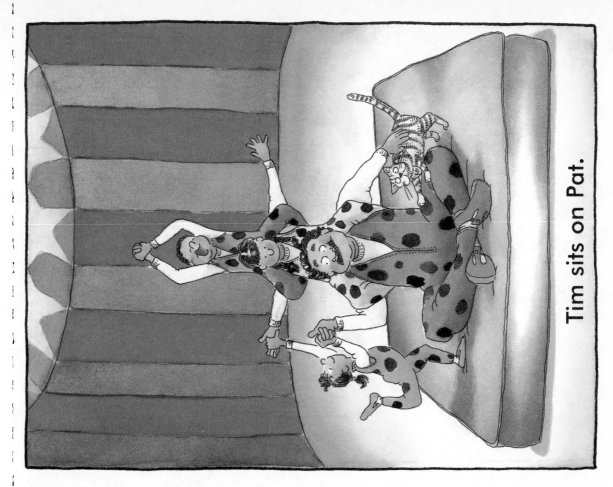

Tim sits on Pat.

5

Pat spins a tin pan.

12

6

Nan sits on Tim.

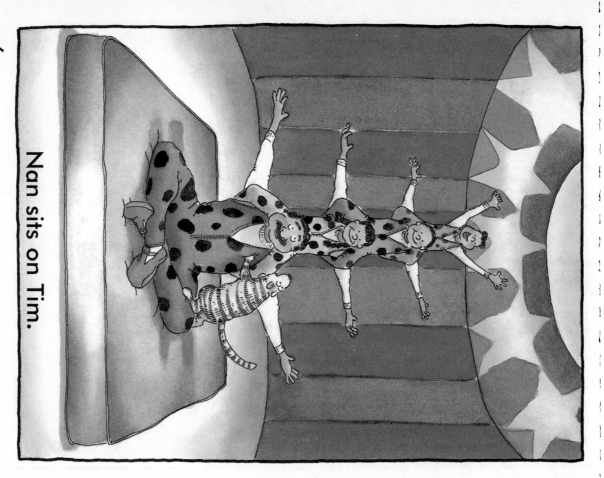

The Pans

Sam has a tin pan.
Sam spins his pan.

11

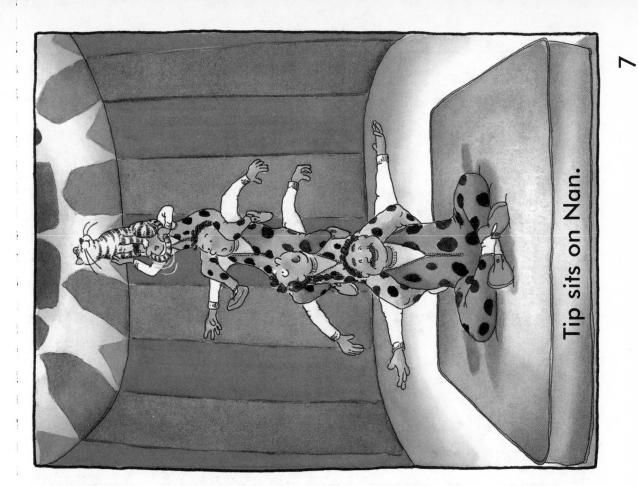

Tip sits on Nan.

7

10

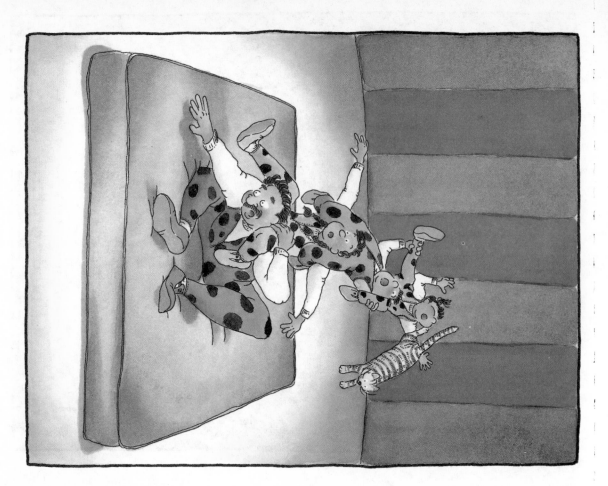

Dan Spins

SRA Open Court Reading

by Anne O'Brien
illustrated by Susanne DeMarco

Core Book 14

SRA

A Division of The McGraw-Hill Companies

Columbus, Ohio

Dan is sad.

2

www.sra4kids.com

SRA/McGraw-Hill

A Division of The McGraw-Hill Companies

Printed in the United States of America.

Send all inquiries to:
SRA/McGraw-Hill
8787 Orion Place
Columbus, OH 43240-4027

Dan hits a pit...and sits.

7

Dan spins.

3

Dan spins his hat.

6

4

Dan dips.

Dan has a hat.

5

SRA Open Court Reading

The Spot

by Lucy Shepard
illustrated by Olivia Cole

Core Book 15

SRA

A Division of The McGraw-Hill Companies
Columbus, Ohio

73

Dad mops and Mom pats the spot.

8

Dad mops the spot.

Mom has a pot.

3

Dad has his mop.

6

4

Mom's pot is hot.

5

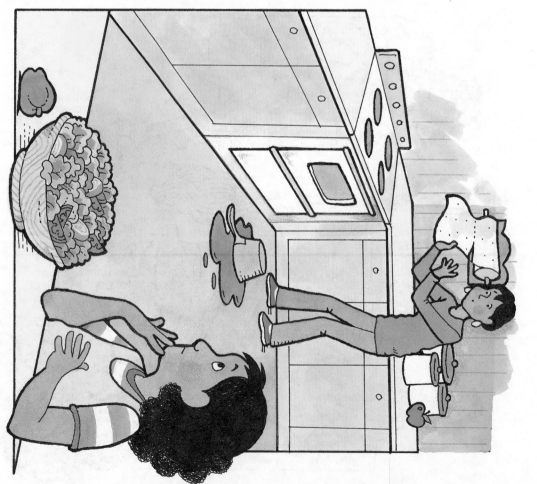

Mom has a spot.

OPEN COURT READING

Bob at Bat

by Nicole Michael
illustrated by Len Epstein

Core Book 16

SRA
A Division of The McGraw-Hill Companies
Columbus, Ohio

Bob pants.

2

Bob bats.

7

Bob is at bat.

3

Bob stands and nods.

6

Bob stamps.

4

Bob taps.

5

The Cab

SRA OPEN COURT READING

by Nancy James
illustrated by Len Epstein

Core Book 17

SRA
A Division of The McGraw-Hill Companies
Columbus, Ohio

The cab stops, and in hops Dan.

8

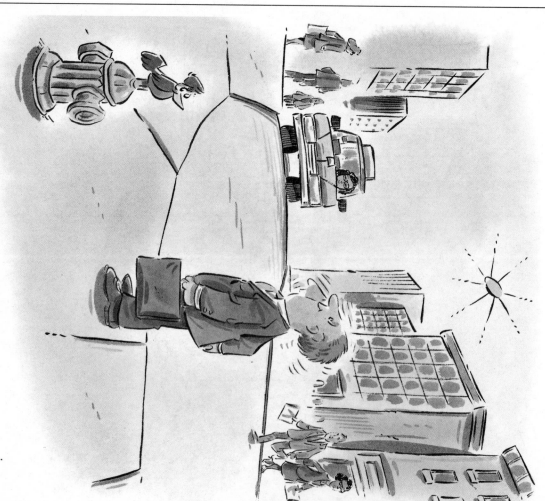

Dan nods.

Dan stands.

3

The cab scats, and Dan taps.

6

4

The cab spins past Dan.

Dan snaps.

5

Sis the Cat

by Mike Dennison
illustrated by Susanne DeMarco

Core Book 18

SRA

A Division of The McGraw-Hill Companies

Columbus, Ohio

I can sit with Sis and Dad.

16

85

Dad is not mad.
And Sis is not sad.

Sis and Dad

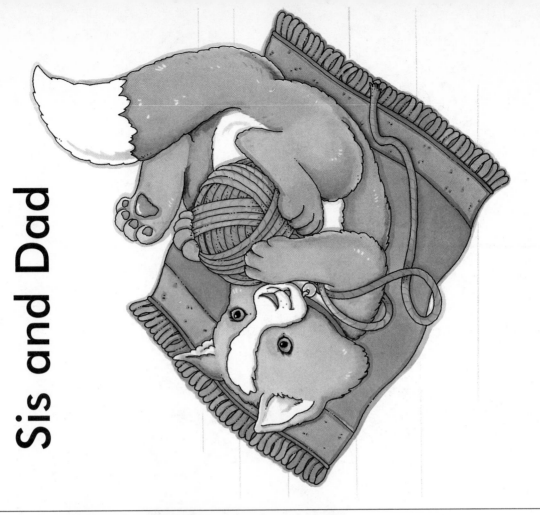

There is Sis. Sis spins and stops on the mat.

3

Dad has Sis.
Sis sits on him.

14

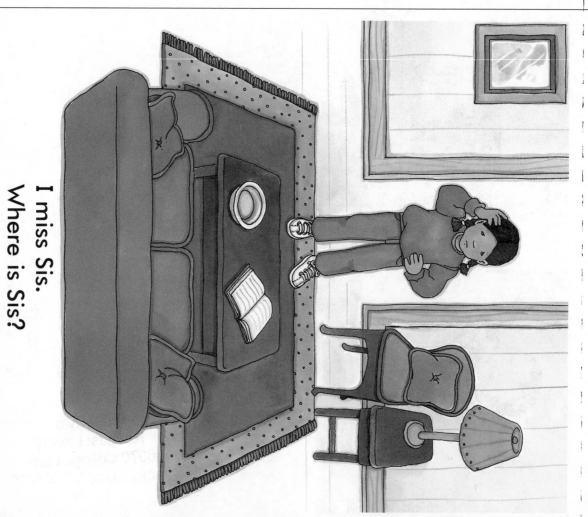

Sis can sit.
Sis can nap.

I miss Sis.
Where is Sis?

Sis can bat.
Sis can tap.

Is Sis with Pam and Bob?
No, Sis is not with Pam and Bob.

12

Sis bats the pans.
Sis hits the hat.

Is Sis in a tin pan?
Sis is not in a tin pan.

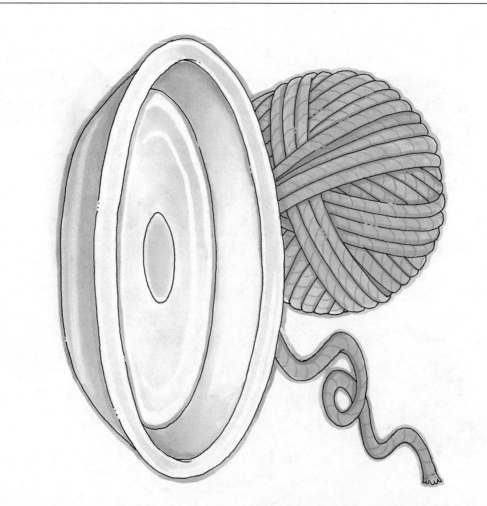

11

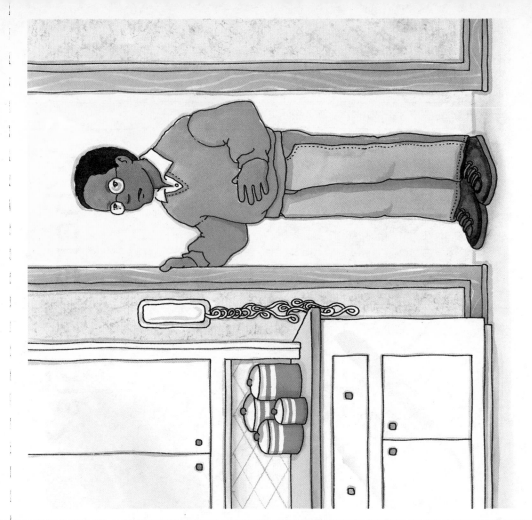

Dad is mad.
Bad cat!

7

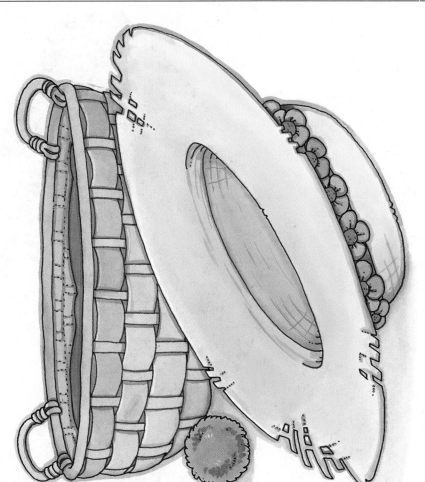

Is Sis in the hat?
Sis is not in the hat.

10

91

Where Is Sis?

Sis scats.
Where is Sis?

8

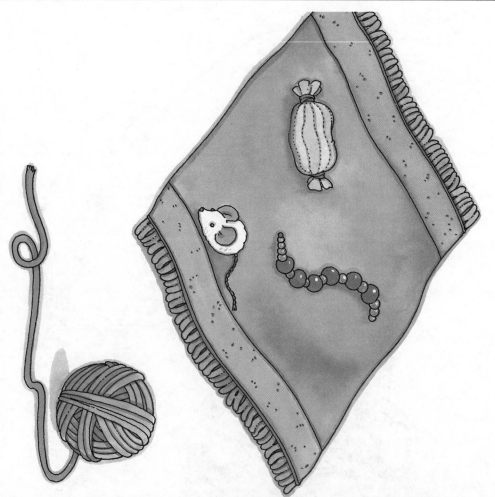

Is Sis on the mat?
Sis is not on the mat.

9

Picnic

SRA Open Court Reading

by Pam Matthews
illustrated by Olivia Cole

Core Book 19

SRA

A Division of The McGraw-Hill Companies

Columbus, Ohio

Dad, Nick, and Pam picnic!

8

93

www.sra4kids.com

SRA/McGraw-Hill

A Division of The McGraw-Hill Companies

Copyright © 2002 by SRA/McGraw-Hill.

Printed in the United States of America.

Send all inquiries to:
SRA/McGraw-Hill
8787 Orion Place
Columbus, OH 43240-4027

2

Pam has the picnic sack.

7

Dad can pick snacks.

3

Nick stands in sand.

6

4

Nick can pack maps.

Pam is in the back.

5

Nat's Nap

by Alice Cary
illustrated by Doug Cushman

Core Book 20

A Division of The McGraw-Hill Companies

Columbus, Ohio

Nat naps in his crib!

8

www.sra4kids.com

SRA/McGraw-Hill

A Division of The McGraw-Hill Companies

Copyright © 2002 by SRA/McGraw-Hill.

All rights reserved. Except as permitted under the United States
Copyright Act, no part of this publication may be reproduced or
distributed in any form or by any means, or stored in a database
or retrieval system, without prior written permission from the
publisher.

Printed in the United States of America.

Send all inquiries to:
SRA/McGraw-Hill
8787 Orion Place
Columbus, OH 43240-4027

2

7

3

6

Ron on the Run

by Alice Cary
illustrated by Olivia Cole

Core Book 21

A Division of The McGraw-Hill Companies

Columbus, Ohio

101

The bus runs on,
but Ron sits and does not run.

8

www.sra4kids.com

SRA/McGraw-Hill

A Division of The McGraw-Hill Companies

Copyright © 2002 by SRA/McGraw-Hill.

Printed in the United States of America.

Send all inquiries to:
SRA/McGraw-Hill
8787 Orion Place
Columbus, OH 43240-4027

2

Ron runs for the bus.
The bus hits mud.
Ron sits in muck.

7

The sun is up.
Ron is on the run.

3

A dump truck hits mud.
Mud hits Ron.
Ron runs and runs.

6

Ron mops and dusts his hut.
Ron hums as he dusts and mops.

4

With his cup and his bun,
Ron is back on the run.

5

SRA Open Court Reading

OPEN COURT READING

The Bug

by Janet Klausner
illustrated by Deborah Colvin Borgo

Core Book 22

SRA

A Division of The McGraw-Hill Companies
Columbus, Ohio

: But is the bug big?

: Big bugs bump in big bags.

www.sra4kids.com

SRA/McGraw-Hill

A Division of The McGraw-Hill Companies

Copyright © 2002 by SRA/McGraw-Hill.

Send all inquiries to:
SRA/McGraw-Hill
8787 Orion Place
Columbus, OH 43240-4027

2

: Not the bag! Is a big bug in the big bag?

: A big bag has the big bug.

: What is in the bag?

: A bug.

3

: Yes. Is the bug in the bag big?

: It is a big bug bag.

6

 : Is it big?

: The bug bag is big.

 : No! Is the bug big?

: In the big bag?

SRA Open Court Reading

Sinbad the Pig

by Anne and Robert O'Brien
illustrated by Meg McLean

Core Book 23

A Division of The McGraw-Hill Companies

Columbus, Ohio

"Sinbad has bad habits!" says Ann.

16

www.sra4kids.com

SRA/McGraw-Hill

A Division of The McGraw-Hill Companies

Copyright © 2002 by SRA/McGraw-Hill.

Printed in the United States of America.

Send all inquiries to:
SRA/McGraw-Hill
8787 Orion Place
Columbus, OH 43240-4027

2

Ann stamps.
Gramps grins.
Sinbad naps.

15

Sinbad Scats

3

Ann trips on Sinbad.

14

111

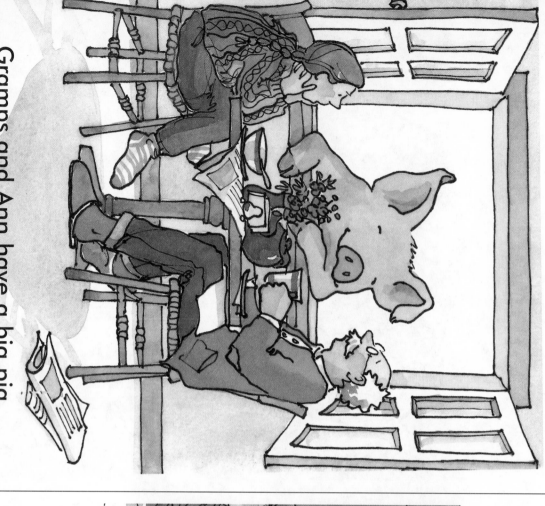

4

Gramps and Ann have a big pig.

13

Sinbad stops and sits back.

The pig is Sinbad.
Sinbad has bad habits.

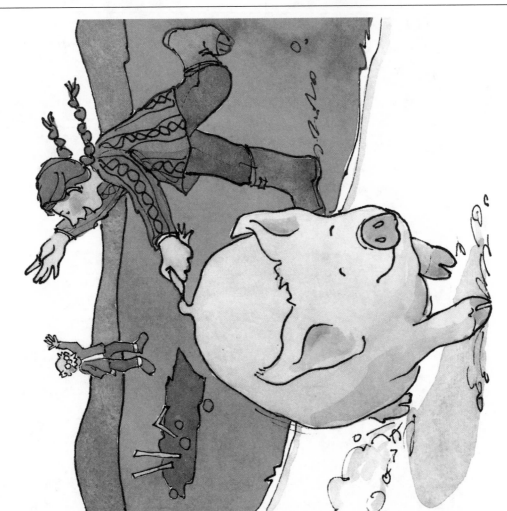

"I got him!" says Ann.

12

Sinbad bumps Gramps.

6

Ann grabs at Sinbad.
Gramps grins.

11

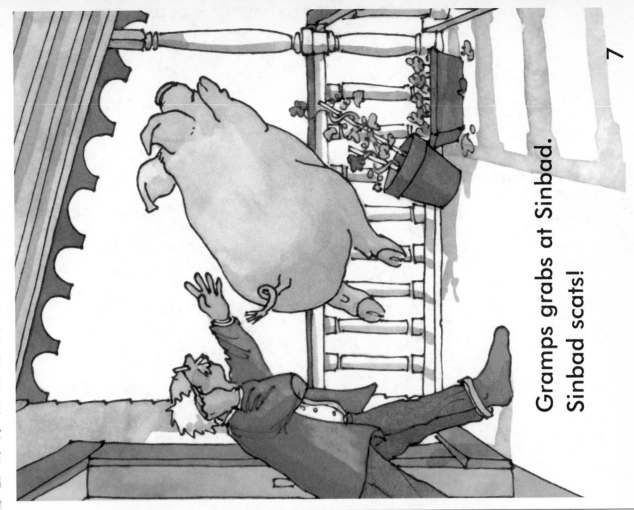

Gramps grabs at Sinbad.
Sinbad scats!

Sinbad runs.
He spins past Ann.

10

Sinbad and Ann

"Grab Sinbad, Ann!" says Gramps.

SRA OPEN COURT READING

Jan and Jack

by Amy Goldman Koss
illustrated by Olivia Cole

Core Book 24

SRA

A Division of The McGraw-Hill Companies

Columbus, Ohio

117

"Jan, I am glad for snacks and a nap."
Jack sits and has his snacks.

8

www.sra4kids.com

SRA/McGraw-Hill

A Division of The McGraw-Hill Companies

Copyright © 2002 by SRA/McGraw-Hill.

Printed in the United States of America.

Send all inquiries to:
SRA/McGraw-Hill
8787 Orion Place
Columbus, OH 43240-4027

2

Jan jabs and jiggles Jack.
"Jan, I had to sit and nap," said Jack.

7

Jan packs Jack's snack.
Jan puts his snack in a jug.

3

Jack naps.

6

Jan tosses the jug in Jack's backpack.
Jan jogs up hills.
She jogs in grass and mud.

4

Jan runs and jumps a plant.

5

SRA Open Court Reading

A Badge

by Ann Ball
illustrated by Meryl Henderson

Core Book 25

SRA
A Division of The McGraw-Hill Companies
Columbus, Ohio

Midge and Madge get a badge.
Midge and Madge hug a judge.

8

Mom is a judge.
Mom can judge.

Midge wants a badge.
So does Madge.

Can Madge get a badge?

Nudge, nudge, nudge.
Nudge, nudge, nudge.
Who gets a badge?

4

Can Midge get a badge?

5

Brad's Ram

by Amy Goldman Koss
illustrated by Len Epstein

Core Book 26

A Division of The McGraw-Hill Companies

Columbus, Ohio

Brad is a trim man.
He has a fat ram.
The ram has a fat hat.

2

Snap! Brad's hat flips up!

7

Brad is a trim man.
Brad's trim hat fits him.
Brad has a fat ram.

3

Brad's ram tugs and tugs.

6

Brad's rain spins fast and nabs his hat.
Brad is mad.
Brad nabs his hat.

4

Brad pulls, stamps, and pants.

5

129

Boris, Doris, and Norm

by Nick Blake
illustrated by Meryl Henderson

Core Book 27

A Division of The McGraw-Hill Companies

Columbus, Ohio

Norm got a brand new crib.
It was not worn and torn.

8

2

Mom and Dad did not have a crib for Norm.

7

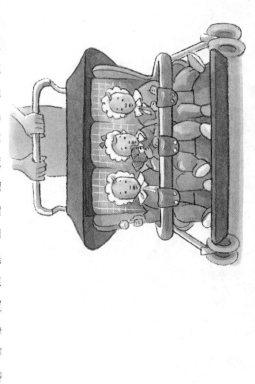

131

Boris, Doris, and Norm are triplets.
Boris, Doris, and Norm were born
in a storm.

3

Mom and Dad put Doris in Mom's old crib.
Mom's old crib was worn and torn.

6

Boris was born first.
After Boris, Doris was born.
After Doris, Norm was born.

4

Mom and Dad put Boris in Dad's old crib.
Dad's old crib was worn and torn.

5

133

SRA Open Court Reading

Jen's Pen

by Amy Goldman Koss
illustrated by Olivia Cole

Core Book 28

SRA

A Division of The McGraw-Hill Companies

Columbus, Ohio

Ted pulls Jen out.
Ted pets Jen and feeds her.
"I will mend Jen's pen!" Ted says.
And Ted does mend Jen's pen.

8

www.sra4kids.com

SRA/McGraw-Hill

A Division of The McGraw-Hill Companies

Copyright © 2002 by SRA/McGraw-Hill.

All rights reserved. Except as permitted under the United States Copyright Act, no part of this publication may be reproduced or distributed in any form or by any means, or stored in a database or retrieval system, without prior written permission from the publisher.

Printed in the United States of America.

Send all inquiries to:
SRA/McGraw-Hill
8787 Orion Place
Columbus, OH 43240-4027

2

Jen hops on top of the pen.
Jen trips and drops in a bucket.
"Jen is stuck and can't get up!"
laugh the horses.

7

Ted has his hen in a pen.
Ted's hen is Jen.
Jen's pen is a mess.

3

135

"Jen is upset and is on the move!"
snort the pigs as Jen runs past.

6

4

Ted promises to mend Jen's pen.

"I'm fed up!" Jen says.
"Ted said he would mend my pen,
but Ted did not mend it."

5

Best Mom

by Lisa Boggs
illustrated by Kersti Frigell

Core Book 29

A Division of The McGraw-Hill Companies

Columbus, Ohio

Dad handed Tom a pin.
Tom pinned it on Mom.
The pin said BEST MOM.

www.sra4kids.com

SRA/McGraw-Hill

A Division of The McGraw-Hill Companies

Copyright © 2002 by SRA/McGraw-Hill.

All rights reserved. Except as permitted under the United States Copyright Act, no part of this publication may be reproduced or distributed in any form or by any means, or stored in a database or retrieval system, without prior written permission from the publisher.

Printed in the United States of America.

Send all inquiries to:
SRA/McGraw-Hill
8787 Orion Place
Columbus, OH 43240-4027

2

Dad landed.
Mom picked him up.

7

139

Tom slipped.
Mom helped him.

3

Tom acted.
Mom clapped.

6

4

Pam spilled it.
Mom mopped it.

Mom patted Pam.
Pam napped.

5

SRA Open Court Reading

Jeff's Job

by Greg Sutton
illustrated by Meryl Henderson

Core Book 30

SRA

A Division of *The McGraw-Hill Companies*

Columbus, Ohio

Jeff and his staff have fun!

www.sra4kids.com

SRA/McGraw-Hill

A Division of The McGraw-Hill Companies

Copyright © 2002 by SRA/McGraw-Hill.

Send all inquiries to:
SRA/McGraw-Hill
8787 Orion Place
Columbus, OH 43240-4027

Jeff and his staff are on the job.

Jeff is on the job.

3

Jeff has a staff.
The staff helps Jeff.

6

143

4

Jeff's job is on a cliff.

Jeff's job is fun.
Jeff's job is a lot of work.
Jeff huffs and puffs.

5

SRA Open Court Reading

A Fox and His Box

by Marj Milano

illustrated by Deborah Colvin Borgo

Core Book 31

SRA

A Division of The McGraw-Hill Companies

Columbus, Ohio

"Yes," said Fox,
"and it did not trap you!"

8

"It can trap rabbits?" said Rabbit.
"But I am a fast rabbit! It cannot trap
fast rabbits!"

Rabbit and Fox sat on Fox's big box.
"You have a big box," said Rabbit.
"Yes!" snapped Fox. "It is a trap!"

"Can it trap an ox?" said Rabbit.
"It cannot trap an ox," said Fox,
"but it can trap rabbits."

4

"Can it trap dogs?" said Rabbit.
"It can trap dogs," said Fox.

"Can it trap cats?" said Rabbit.
"It can trap cats," said Fox.

5

SRA Open Court Reading

Zack the One-Man Band

by Diane Zaga
illustrated by Len Epstein

Core Book 32

SRA

A Division of The McGraw-Hill Companies

Columbus, Ohio

"Do not fuss," added Zack.
"Grab tin pots! Grab small sticks!
Start a grand band!"
Zack and his band
got back on his red bus.

8

www.sra4kids.com

SRA/McGraw-Hill

A Division of The McGraw-Hill Companies

Copyright © 2002 by SRA/McGraw-Hill.

Printed in the United States of America.

Send all inquiries to:
SRA/McGraw-Hill
8787 Orion Place
Columbus, OH 43240-4027

Zack huffed and puffed.
"I must stop," he panted.

Gus and Cass sat on rocks.
ZAP! POP! SNAP!
"What is it?" said Cass.

3

151

BAM! ZAP! BOP!
Zack's band started up.
"Zack, you are a grand band!" called Cass.

6

"A big red bus has zipped up. It has a man and a big brass band," said Gus.

4

The man on the red bus blasted, "I am Zack the One-Man Band, and here is my big brass band!"

5

SRA Open Court Reading

Bizz Buzz

by Michael P. Fertig
illustrated by Meryl Henderson

Core Book 33

SRA
A Division of The McGraw-Hill Companies
Columbus, Ohio

It is jazz!
It is a jazz band.
A jazz band is fun!

2

Yes!

7

Is it a buzz?
It is a big buzz.

3

Can it be Dad?
It is not Dad.

6

Is it a fizz?
Buzz, fizz.
What is it?

Bizz, bizz.
Buzz, fizz.
Bop! Bam!

SRA Open Court Reading

Dogs and Cats

by Michael P. Fertig
illustrated by Loretta Lustig

Core Book 34

SRA

A Division of The McGraw-Hill Companies

Columbus, Ohio

Figs, Mugs, Bugs, and Bigs all like Sam.

8

www.sra4kids.com

SRA/McGraw-Hill

A Division of The McGraw-Hill Companies

Copyright © 2002 by SRA/McGraw-Hill.

Printed in the United States of America.

Send all inquiries to:
SRA/McGraw-Hill
8787 Orion Place
Columbus, OH 43240-4027

2

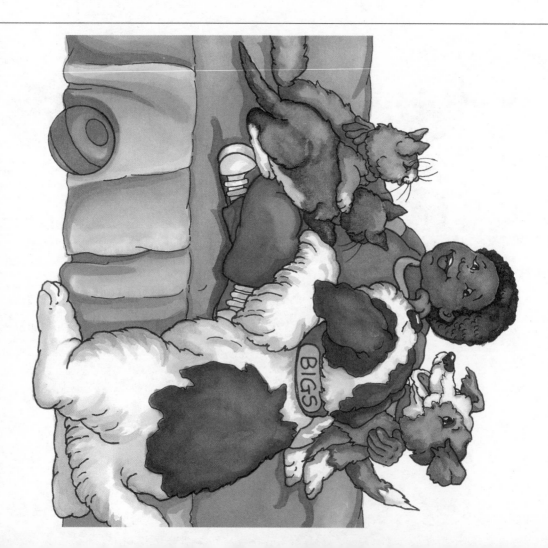

Sam hugs Figs, Mugs, Bugs, and Bigs.

7

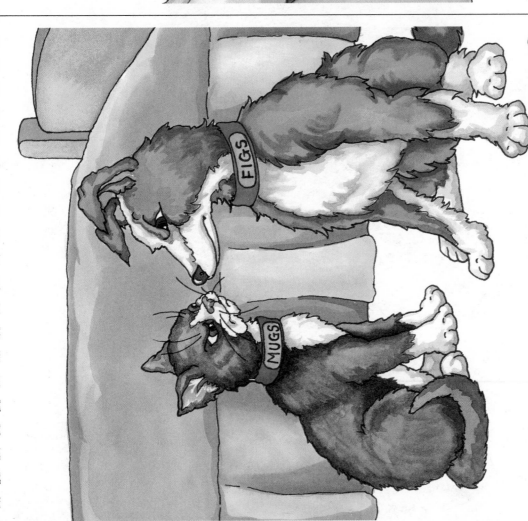

Sam has dogs.
His dogs are Bigs and Figs.

3

Mugs does not like Figs.
Figs does not like Mugs.

6

4

Sam has cats.
His cats are Bugs and Mugs.

Bigs does not like Bugs.
Bugs does not like Bigs.

5

161

SRA
OPEN COURT
READING

Jen Dreamt

by Bill Dennis
illustrated by Olivia Cole

Core Book 35

SRA

A Division of The McGraw-Hill Companies

Columbus, Ohio

Jen lifted her head and leapt from her bed.
"Mom, can I get bread at breakfast? Can I
spread jam on my bread?"

8

Jen dreamt her bed was good bread.

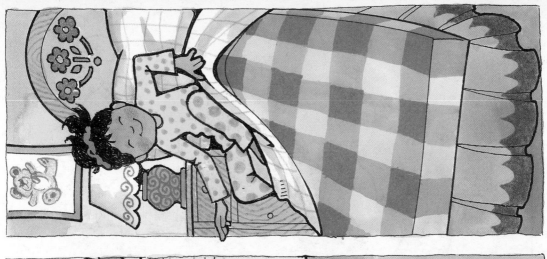

Jen had bread and went to bed.

3

Jen dreamt she spread jam
on her bed.

6

163

Jen dreamt her bed was made of bread.

4

Can I dab bread in milk?
Or can I spread jam on it instead?

5

OPEN COURT READING

Run and Pass

by Nick Ball
illustrated by Gary Undercuffler

Core Book 36

A Division of The McGraw-Hill Companies

Columbus, Ohio

Greg runs, and Ted misses.
Ted is impressed.

8

www.sra4kids.com

SRA/McGraw-Hill

A Division of The McGraw-Hill Companies

Copyright © 2002 by SRA/McGraw-Hill.

All rights reserved. Except as permitted under the United States Copyright Act, no part of this publication may be reproduced or distributed in any form or by any means, or stored in a database or retrieval system, without prior written permission from the publisher.

Printed in the United States of America.

Send all inquiries to:
SRA/McGraw-Hill
8787 Orion Place
Columbus, OH 43240-4027

2

But Bob is not stressed.
Bob can run and pass.

7

166

Bob can pass a ball.
The ball crosses the grass.

3

Ted is not impressed.
Ted is dressed to play.
Ted will cross the grass and run at Bob.

6

Bob can toss the ball to Greg.
Greg runs and crosses the grass.

4

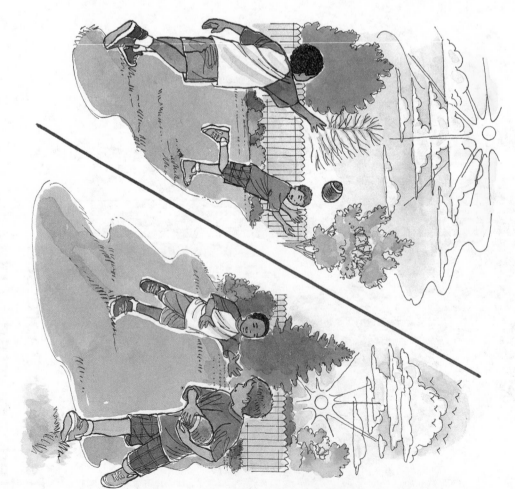

Bob and Greg run and pass.

5

Trash

by Amy Goldman Koss
illustrated by Len Epstein

Core Book 37

A Division of The McGraw-Hill Companies

Columbus, Ohio

Mick put his trash stack in the small shed.

8

2

five old comic books,
a crushed red drum set,
and half a smashed sled.

7

Mick had trash stacks:
dented and bent tin cans,

3

four fishnet strips,
torn flag scraps,

6

cut and split logs,
two smashed beds,

three cracked dishes,
small bits of crashed ships,

Seth's Bath

SRA Open Court Reading

by Anne O'Brien
illustrated by Gary Undercuffler

Core Book 38

SRA

A Division of The McGraw-Hill Companies
Columbus, Ohio

173

"All finished, Seth?" said Dad.
"Yes, Dad," said Seth. "All finished!"

8

www.sra4kids.com

SRA/McGraw-Hill

A Division of The McGraw-Hill Companies

Copyright © 2002 by SRA/McGraw-Hill.

All rights reserved. Except as permitted under the United States Copyright Act, no part of this publication may be reproduced or distributed in any form or by any means, or stored in a database or retrieval system, without prior written permission from the publisher.

Printed in the United States of America.

Send all inquiries to:
SRA/McGraw-Hill
8787 Orion Place
Columbus, OH 43240-4027

2

"Thick fog!
Jump ship!"

SRA Open Court Reading

Seth stepped into his bathtub.
"Must get to the ship!"

3

"The ship has thumped and hit big rocks.
Get the rafts!"

6

175

4

"Cast off!" called Seth.
"All hands on deck!"

"Rocks in the water!
Man the ship's masts!"

5

The Children Get a Rabbit

by Rob Hip
illustrated by Barry Mullins

Core Book 39

SRA

A Division of The McGraw-Hill Companies

Columbus, Ohio

The children and the rabbit
get back in the truck.
Ellen and Dillon had fun with Dad!

8

Dad and the children get melon for a snack.
The rabbit has a carrot.

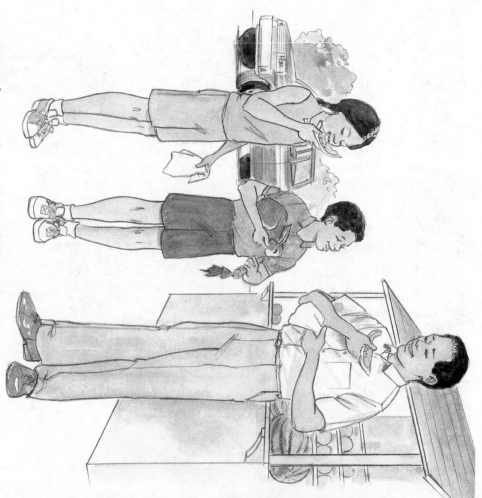

7

Dad and the children get in the truck.
This will be a fun trip for Ellen and Dillon!

3

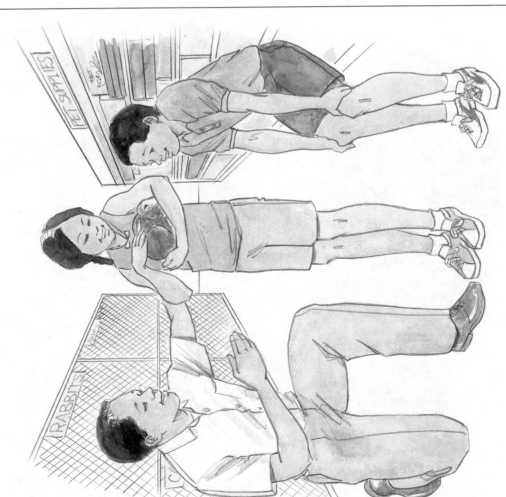

Ellen and Dillon pet the rabbit.
"Dad, can I adopt him?"

6

The children think the animals are fun.
That animal has a banana.

4

The children see the big panda.
"Dad, is that animal an opossum?"

5

SRA
OPEN COURT
READING

Panda Band

by Alice Cary
illustrated by Roz Schanzer

Core Book 40

A Division of The McGraw-Hill Companies
Columbus, Ohio

Amanda Panda has Tom Cat's brass sax,
a big band, and lots of fans.
"You are tops!" Mom and Pop tell
Amanda.

16

2

Both Zack and Max drop in.
"Let's be a big band!" says Amanda Panda.

"Oh, no! More racket!" think Mom and Pop.

15

Amanda's Sax

"Sax racket!" mumbles Mom.

"Sax racket!" grumbles Pop.

14

Amanda Panda mops at Tom
Cat's Jazz Club.
She pushes a damp mop.

4

"Mom! Pop!" calls Amanda.
"I got Tom Cat's brass sax!"

13

Amanda stops.
"I can't stand this,"
she thunders.

5

Amanda's Band

12

6

"I am hot and a mess.
I think this job must stop!"

"I got Tom Cat's brass sax!
I can drop the damp mop
and be tops!"

11

Amanda sees Tom Cat and his brass sax.
She has a wish.

7

"This brass sax?"
"Yes, this brass sax!"

10

8

"Tom Cat," Amanda grumbles,
"you do not have to push a mop.
You have a brass sax,
a big band, and lots of fans."

Tom Cat tosses Amanda his brass sax.
"Hush," he tells Amanda Panda.
"I can fix things for you.
Have this brass sax!"

9

189

SRA Open Court Reading

Chuck's Chest

by Sharon Blake
illustrated by Len Epstein

Core Book 41

SRA

A Division of The McGraw-Hill Companies

Columbus, Ohio

It is a lunch.
Chuck's lunch is in the chest.

8

www.sra4kids.com

SRA/McGraw-Hill

A Division of The McGraw-Hill Companies

Copyright © 2002 by SRA/McGraw-Hill.

Printed in the United States of America.

Send all inquiries to:
SRA/McGraw-Hill
8787 Orion Place
Columbus, OH 43240-4027

2

"Chad, check in the chest.
There is not much."

7

What is in this chest?
Is Chuck rich?

6

That is Chuck.
This is his chest.

3

4

I cannot lift this chest.
What is in this chest?

Is it a bunch of cash?

5

Patch Gets the Ball

by Anne O'Brien
illustrated by Meryl Henderson

Core Book 42

SRA

A Division of The McGraw-Hill Companies

Columbus, Ohio

"Let's do this.
Chuck can hit.
I will pitch.
Lil can catch,
and Patch can fetch!"

8

www.sra4kids.com

SRA/McGraw-Hill

A Division of The McGraw-Hill Companies

Copyright © 2002 by SRA/McGraw-Hill.

Printed in the United States of America.

Send all inquiries to:
SRA/McGraw-Hill
8787 Orion Place
Columbus, OH 43240-4027

2

Patch ran past tall grass.
He ran past plants
and into the ditch.
Patch fetched the ball.

Lil, Midge, and Chuck met
at Chestnut Ridge Ball Park.
Midge pitched the ball,
and Lil hit it.
Midge ran after the ball
and tossed it to Chuck.

3

"Patch!" Midge called for her dog.
"Fetch the ball, Patch!"

6

"Let's switch," said Chuck.
Chuck can pitch,
Midge can hit, and
Lil can catch.
Midge hit the pitched ball.
"I'll catch it!" called Chuck.

But the ball went past Chuck,
past tall grass, past plants,
and landed in a ditch.

Grab a Star

by Dottie Raymer

illustrated by Gary Undercuffler

Core Book 43

SRA

A Division of The McGraw-Hill Companies

Columbus, Ohio

"I can catch stars!" said Max.

"Mom, you are smart!"

8

www.sra4kids.com

SRA/McGraw-Hill

A Division of The McGraw-Hill Companies

Copyright © 2002 by SRA/McGraw-Hill.

All rights reserved. Except as permitted under the United States Copyright Act, no part of this publication may be reproduced or distributed in any form or by any means, or stored in a database or retrieval system, without prior written permission from the publisher.

Printed in the United States of America.

Send all inquiries to:
SRA/McGraw-Hill
8787 Orion Place
Columbus, OH 43240-4027

"Max," called Mom.
"This is a star you can catch!"

"Mom, are stars far off?" asked Max.
"Yes, Max," said Mom.
"Stars are far, far away."

3

Max said, "Stars are so far.
I can't have stars."

6

"Mom, can I grab stars for fun?"
asked Max.

"Hmmm...grab stars for fun...," said Mom.

4

"Sit here, Max," added Mom.

"You can catch stars for fun."

5

OPEN COURT READING

A Lamb on a Limb

by Jan Stewart

illustrated by Pat Lucas-Morris

Core Book 44

A Division of The McGraw-Hill Companies

Columbus, Ohio

Dad will get the lamb off the limb.

8

www.sra4kids.com

SRA/McGraw-Hill

A Division of *The McGraw-Hill Companies*

Copyright © 2002 by SRA/McGraw-Hill.

Printed in the United States of America.

Send all inquiries to:
SRA/McGraw-Hill
8787 Orion Place
Columbus, OH 43240-4027

Crumbs will not get the lamb off the limb. The lamb is a stuffed lamb!

Is that a lamb up there?

3

The thumb did not get the lamb
off the limb. Will crumbs get the
lamb off the limb?

6

How did that lamb get on the limb?

4

How can the children get the lamb off the limb? Will a thumb get the lamb off the limb?

5

SRA
OPEN COURT
READING

Wendell's Pets

by Anne and Robert O'Brien
illustrated by Ellen Joy Sasaki

Core Book 45

SRA

A Division of The McGraw-Hill Companies

Columbus, Ohio

"Here!" said Wendell.
"With me!"
And Wendell's pets sat with him!

8

2

Wendell's pets hopped, scratched, and wiggled.
"Wendell, you will have to put your pets away," said Mr. Webb.

7

Wendell's Pets

3

Wendell's pets went to his class,
and his class was glad.
But Mr. Webb was not glad.

6

Wendell had lots of pets.
Wendell had his cat and his duck.

4

Wendell had his rabbit and his lizard.
Wendell had frogs and a tub for his bugs.

5

SRA Open Court Reading

SRA Open Court Reading

The Whiz

by Mark Decker
illustrated by Len Epstein

Core Book 46

SRA
A Division of The McGraw-Hill Companies
Columbus, Ohio

Wham! When the Whiz stops, it stops fast.
Will you ride the Whiz?

8

www.sra4kids.com

SRA/McGraw-Hill

A Division of The McGraw-Hill Companies

Copyright © 2002 by SRA/McGraw-Hill.

Printed in the United States of America.

Send all inquiries to:
SRA/McGraw-Hill
8787 Orion Place
Columbus, OH 43240-4027

The Whiz whips up a big hill.
Then it whips past a bridge.

7

This is the Whiz.

3

211

When it starts, the Whiz drops fast and far.
Wham! The Whiz whips left.
Wham! The Whiz whips back.

6

When the Whiz starts, it chugs up and up.

4

When it is at the top, the Whiz stops.

5

SRA
OPEN COURT READING

Garden Sisters

by Ann West
illustrated by Olivia Cole

Core Book 47

SRA

A Division of The McGraw-Hill Companies

Columbus, Ohio

"In the summer, Amber can plant big
ferns," Mom said. "Jennifer can plant
big ferns in the garden."
Jennifer and Amber felt better.
They like summer.

8

www.sra4kids.com

SRA/McGraw-Hill

A Division of The McGraw-Hill Companies

Copyright © 2002 by SRA/McGraw-Hill.

Send all inquiries to:
SRA/McGraw-Hill
8787 Orion Place
Columbus, OH 43240-4027

"I want to plant big ferns," Amber said.
"In the summer, I will plant big ferns."

214

SRA Open Court Reading

This is Jennifer and her sister Amber.
Jennifer and Amber have a garden.
Jennifer and Amber are garden partners.

3

"It is winter and the garden is white," said Mom.

6

4

The sisters like plants.
Mom is a gardener.
Jennifer and Amber are Mom's
garden helpers.

"I wonder, can we plant big ferns in
the garden?" asked Jennifer.
Mom said, "Yes, in the summer."

5

Open Court Reading

Whir and Stir

by Patricia Griffith
illustrated by Len Epstein

Core Book 48

SRA
A Division of The McGraw-Hill Companies
Columbus, Ohio

"Have a glass of fresh milk, Irwin.
Now it is carrot bread," said Dad.
"Carrot bread! Good!"

8

www.sra4kids.com

SRA/McGraw-Hill

A Division of The McGraw-Hill Companies

Copyright © 2002 by SRA/McGraw-Hill.

All rights reserved. Except as permitted under the United States Copyright Act, no part of this publication may be reproduced or distributed in any form or by any means, or stored in a database or retrieval system, without prior written permission from the publisher.

Printed in the United States of America.

Send all inquiries to:
SRA/McGraw-Hill
8787 Orion Place
Columbus, OH 43240-4027

2

"It was eggs and butter
and nuts and carrots.
What is it now, Dad?
Is it finished?"

7

Dad picked up his mixer.
"Pass the butter, Irwin,"
said Dad, "and let's stir in fresh milk."

3

219

Dad put carrots and nuts in his mixer.
WHIR!
"What is it?" wondered Irwin.
"Pass the pan, Irwin," said Dad.
"We can put this batter in it."

6

Dad put butter and milk in his mixer.
WHIR!
"What is it?" wondered Irwin.
"Hand me eggs, Irwin," Dad said,
"and let's stir in a little salt."

4

Dad put eggs and salt in his mixer.
WHIR!
"What is it?" wondered Irwin.
"Pass the carrots, Irwin," said Dad.
"We will stir in nuts, too."

5

SRA Open Court Reading

A Blur with Fur

by Chris Mathews
illustrated by Mark Corcoran

Core Book 49

SRA

A Division of The McGraw-Hill Companies

Columbus, Ohio

It is Burt.
The blur with fur is Burt.

8

www.sra4kids.com

SRA/McGraw-Hill

A Division of The McGraw-Hill Companies

Copyright © 2002 by SRA/McGraw-Hill.

Send all inquiries to:
SRA/McGraw-Hill
8787 Orion Place
Columbus, OH 43240-4027

"What is that blur with fur?" asked Arthur.

A blur with fur crossed the carpet.

3

The blur with fur dashed and crashed.
It curled and twirled.

6

A blur with fur ran and crossed the curb.

4

A blur with fur ran so fast, it turned a corner and left tracks in the grass.

5

Chirp and Scat

by Toby Gates
illustrated by Len Epstein

Core Book 50

SRA

A Division of The McGraw-Hill Companies

Columbus, Ohio

Chirp missed that impish little cat.
Now Chirp spends time with his
best pal, Scat.

16

www.sra4kids.com

SRA/McGraw-Hill

A Division of The McGraw-Hill Companies

Copyright © 2002 by SRA/McGraw-Hill.

All rights reserved. Except as permitted under the United States Copyright Act, no part of this publication may be reproduced or distributed in any form or by any means, or stored in a database or retrieval system, without prior written permission from the publisher.

Printed in the United States of America.

Send all inquiries to:
SRA/McGraw-Hill
8787 Orion Place
Columbus, OH 43240-4027

Chirp admitted that he'd not been fair, and Chirp felt bad that Scat was put out there.

Scat Moves In

Chirp is a bird.
Scat is a cat.
Chirp and Scat live with Robert and Barbara Platt.

3

"Scat, that's it. Get out!" Robert said.
Then Chirp felt bad.
In fact Chirp felt sad.
Scat whimpered and got up from his soft bed.

14

The wind whipped fast and hard when Scat turned up on Platt's big branch.

4

Next Chirp tugged and scratched at Platt's rug. The Platts stepped in and spotted Scat, all snug.

13

Scat was such an impish little cat.
Robert and Barbara called him Scat.

5

Chirp was glad his plan had worked.
Chirp jumped, fluttered, and chirped.

12

Scat turned fast for such an impish cat.
Robert and Barbara loved Scat's purr
when they sat.

6

Robert hollered at Scat for the scratch
on Barbara's chair.
Scat was sad and felt this was not fair.

11

231

Robert and Barbara could not tell
that Chirp did not like Scat very well.

7

Chirp flipped his latch back and sat on
his perch.
Chirp laughed at Scat left there in a lurch.

10

Did Barbara and Robert forget Chirp at last?
Chirp felt that Scat must exit rather fast!

8

Chirp's Plan

Chirp started his plan and lifted his latch.
Chirp went to Barbara's chair and
scratched at the patch.

9

Little Pat

by Bob Parker
illustrated by Len Epstein

Core Book 51

A Division of The McGraw-Hill Companies

Columbus, Ohio

233

Big purple men did not stop little Pat.
Little Pat is a big star.

8

2

Big purple men cannot tackle little Pat.

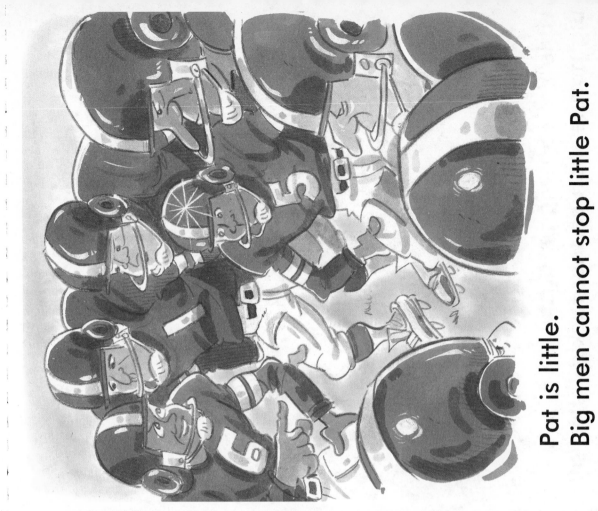

Pat is little.
Big men cannot stop little Pat.

3

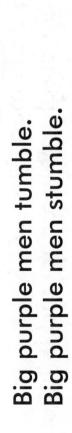

Big purple men tumble.
Big purple men stumble.

6

Little Pat can wiggle past.
Big purple men cannot tackle little Pat.

4

Little Pat can scramble over big purple men.
Big purple men cannot tackle little Pat.

5

Just a Nickel

by Don Best
illustrated by Kersti Frigell

Core Book 52

A Division of The McGraw-Hill Companies

Columbus, Ohio

It is just a nickel for a nap.
Dad can get a nap for a nickel.

8

237

It is just a nickel to hop
on a jet.
The children can hop on
a jet for a nickel.

It is just a nickel to have fun.
The children can have fun for a nickel.

3

It is just a nickel to see "Hansel and Gretel."
The children can see "Hansel and Gretel" for a nickel.

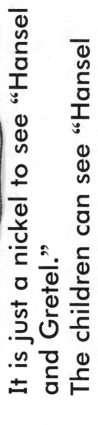

6

It is just a nickel to go in a tunnel.
The children can go in a tunnel
for a nickel.

4

It is just a nickel to hop
on a camel.
The children can hop on
a camel for a nickel.

5

Kim tramped on grass and trudged up hills.
But that fat skunk had a picnic lunch!

8

Kim's Trip

by Alice Cary
illustrated by Meryl Henderson

Core Book 53

A Division of The McGraw·Hill Companies

Columbus, Ohio

www.sra4kids.com

SRA/McGraw-Hill

A Division of The McGraw-Hill Companies

Copyright © 2002 by SRA/McGraw-Hill.

Send all inquiries to:
SRA/McGraw-Hill
8787 Orion Place
Columbus, OH 43240-4027

2

Kim tracked that dark skunk.
It sat and munched on her picnic lunch!

7

For the trip, Kim packed park maps, snacks, and a jacket. Kim tramped on grass and trudged up hills.

3

Her backpack! It had no picnic or snack!

6

243

Kim picked a flat spot in Birch Park.
Kim fixed her bag and rested.

4

Kim heard clicks and sharp snaps.
Kim sat up and kept watch.

5

SRA Open Court Reading

Hank the Crank

by Robert O'Brien
illustrated by Len Epstein

Core Book 54

A Division of The McGraw-Hill Companies

Columbus, Ohio

Sheriff Long got the robber.
Farmer Ann got Hank.
Sheriff Long thanked Hank,
but the robber thanked Farmer Ann!

8

2

Hank started banging his head on
the robber's long leg.
Hank flung pebbles at the robber
and ran him up a lamp.

Hank was such a crank.
Hank was honking and hissing
as much as he could.
Hank honked at Farmer Ann.

3

A robber ran out of the bank
and jumped into Farmer Ann's bus!
Hank banged on his box and tipped it over.
Hank honked and sprung from his box.

6

"Hank, I am going to sell you,"
said Farmer Ann.
Hank started honking and hissing
at Farmer Ann.

4

Farmer Ann put Hank in a box
and put it in her bus.
On her way to Mark's Market,
she stopped at a bank.

5

Quinn's Pond

by Stephan Queen
illustrated by Meryl Henderson

Core Book 55

A Division of The McGraw-Hill Companies

Columbus, Ohio

Kids can swim in
Quinn's Pond, too!

www.sra4kids.com

SRA/McGraw-Hill

A Division of The McGraw-Hill Companies

Copyright © 2002 by SRA/McGraw-Hill.

Send all inquiries to:
SRA/McGraw-Hill
8787 Orion Place
Columbus, OH 43240-4027

2

Kids sit by Quinn's Pond, but
cannot catch the quick fish.

7

Lots of animals swim
in Quinn's Pond.

3

Kids plan a picnic.
Mom puts her quilt
on the grass.

6

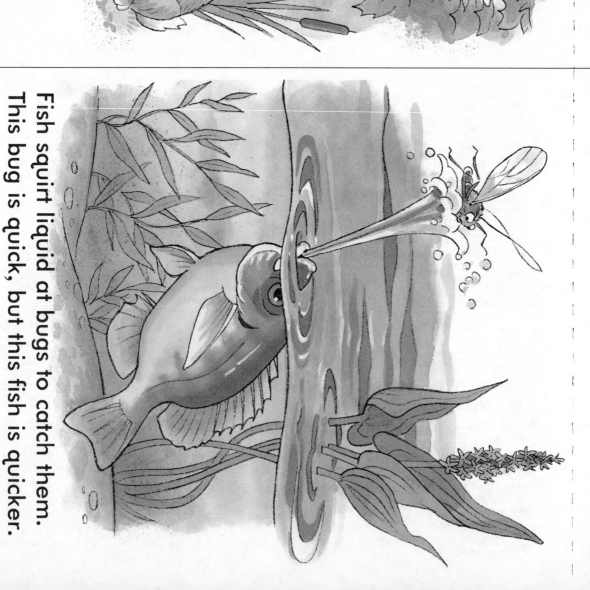

Lots of ducks quack
and quack.
Ducks do not quit and quack
until dark.

4

Fish squirt liquid at bugs to catch them.
This bug is quick, but this fish is quicker.

5

SRA OPEN COURT READING

The Stand

by Alice Cary

illustrated by Kersti Frigell

Core Book 56

SRA

A Division of The McGraw-Hill Companies

Columbus, Ohio

Tess has to rest and nap.
"No problems in my yard at all!"
yawns Tess.

8

253

www.sra4kids.com

SRA/McGraw-Hill

A Division of The McGraw-Hill Companies

Copyright © 2002 by SRA/McGraw-Hill.

All rights reserved. Except as permitted under the United States Copyright Act, no part of this publication may be reproduced or distributed in any form or by any means, or stored in a database or retrieval system, without prior written permission from the publisher.

Printed in the United States of America.

Send all inquiries to:
SRA/McGraw-Hill
8787 Orion Place
Columbus, OH 43240-4027

Deb can't paddle in the pond.
"You are in luck!" says Tess.
"This rubber raft is for you."

7

254

HELP STAND

Tess has a help stand in her yard!
No problem is too big or small.
Tess can help.

3

Carl has no pocket.
"You are in luck!" Tess tells Carl.
"This belt will fit around your middle."
The belt fits, and Carl giggles.

6

T. Rex wants snacks.
"You are in luck!" says Tess.
"Yum, this snack will fill you up."

Greg yanked his neck, and it hurts.
"You are in luck!" Tess tells Greg.
"This scarf of red yarn will help."

4

5

The King
of Purple

by Tim Paulson
illustrated by Kersti Frigell

Core Book 57

A Division of The McGraw-Hill Companies

Columbus, Ohio

Back in his kingdom King Purple asked,
"What color do you like the best?"
His friends said, "We like all colors!
All colors are the best!"

16

www.sra4kids.com

SRA/McGraw-Hill

A Division of The McGraw-Hill Companies

Copyright © 2002 by SRA/McGraw-Hill.

All rights reserved. Except as permitted under the United States Copyright Act, no part of this publication may be reproduced or distributed in any form or by any means, or stored in a database or retrieval system, without prior written permission from the publisher.

Printed in the United States of America.

Send all inquiries to:
SRA/McGraw-Hill
8787 Orion Place
Columbus, OH 43240-4027

King Purple saw a red harp with strings
and a red bell that went "ding!"

King Purple liked purple.
His clothes were purple. His purple bed
had purple quilts.
His pets were purple, too.

3

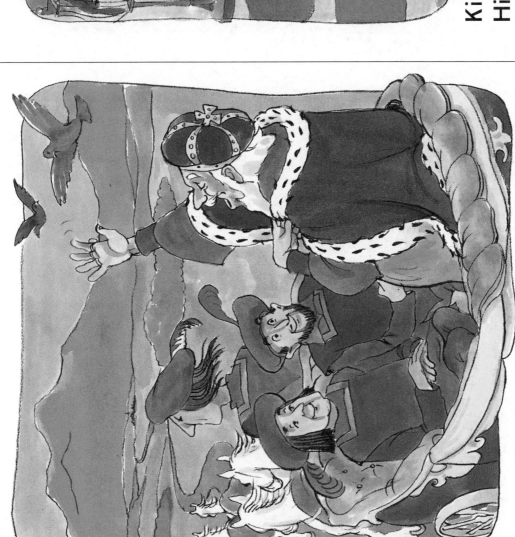

"We will go to the red hills and look for
red things," said King Purple.

14

King Purple liked walking in his garden. He had purple yams and a purple melon in his garden.

The sun was setting when King Purple got back. "Can you tell me what color this is?" he asked. "It is not purple, black, or pink. I think it is red."

261

King Purple liked hunting on his purple yak.
He hunted purple birds, purple squirrels,
and a purple bear.

5

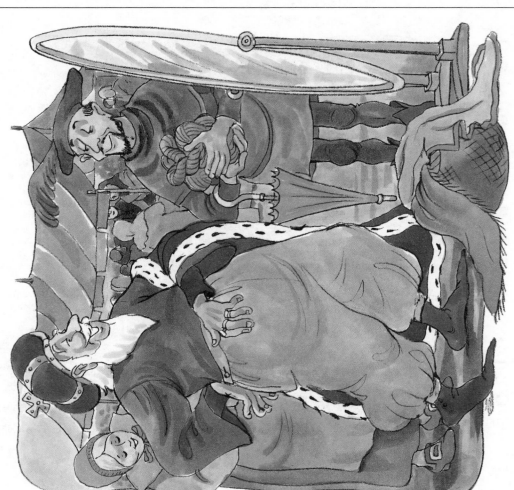

King Purple got pink yarn and pink pants.

12

King Purple liked sitting in his yard and eating purple plums.

6

Then King Purple asked, "Can you tell me what color this is? It is not purple. It is not black. I think it is pink!"

11

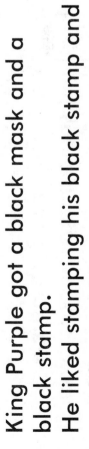

King Purple liked sitting by his pond.
Quacking purple ducks and squirming
purple squid were in his pond.

7

King Purple got a black mask and a
black stamp.
He liked stamping his black stamp and
would not quit!

10

All things in King Purple's Kingdom were purple. Purple, purple, purple, purple!

King Purple had too much purple. "I will get some things that are black," he said.

SRA Open Court Reading

Mason's Big Hat

by Patrick Harris
illustrated by Len Epstein

Core Book 58

A Division of The McGraw-Hill Companies

Columbus, Ohio

Mason rips the label.
Mabel gets a hat.

www.sra4kids.com

SRA/McGraw-Hill

A Division of The McGraw-Hill Companies

Copyright © 2002 by SRA/McGraw-Hill.

All rights reserved. Except as permitted under the United States Copyright Act, no part of this publication may be reproduced or distributed in any form or by any means, or stored in a database or retrieval system, without prior written permission from the publisher.

Printed in the United States of America.

Send all inquiries to:
SRA/McGraw-Hill
8787 Orion Place
Columbus, OH 43240-4027

2

Mason trips on Mabel and hits the table.
Mason dumps the lunch.

7

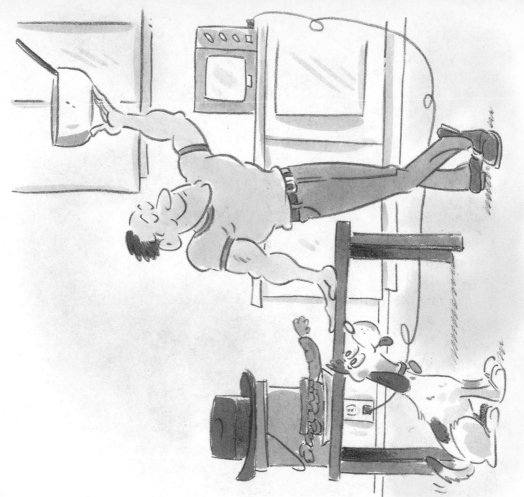

Mason is big.

3

Mason hits the cable and then the ladle.
Mason spills the punch.

6

The label in the hat says BIG.

4

Mason can get it on his head.
But Mason is not able to get the hat off.

5

SRA
OPEN COURT
READING

Gull and Crane

by Helen Byers
illustrated by Deborah Colvin Borgo

Core Book 59

SRA

A Division of *The McGraw-Hill Companies*
Columbus, Ohio

Snake swam back across Lake Cape.

8

2

Gull saw Snake, and she yelled to Crane. "Snake is in Lake Cape! Snake in Lake Cape!"

Gull and Crane are pals.
Gull and Crane waded in Lake Cape.

3

Snake swam across Lake Cape.

6

Gull and Crane fished together in Lake Cape.

4

Snake had a nest across Lake Cape.
He was mad at Crane and Gull.
They ate Snake's fish!

5